21st
Century
Skills Library

ANIMAL INVADERS

SMALL INDIAN MONGOOSE

BARBARA A. SOMERVILL

CHERRY LAKE Publishing

Published in the United States of America by
Cherry Lake Publishing, Ann Arbor, Michigan
www.cherrylakepublishing.com

Content Adviser
Dr. Sarah Simons, Executive Director, Global Invasive Species Programme

Credits
Photos: Cover and page 1, ©Jack Jeffrey Photography; pages 4, 24, and 26, ©Photo
Resource Hawaii/Alamy; page 7, ©Tom Uhlman/Alamy; page 8, ©Christopher
Barnes/Alamy; page 10, ©Bill Waldman/Alamy; page 12, ©Photoshot Holdings
Ltd/Alamy; page 14, ©Bryan Lowry/Alamy; page 17, ©iStockphoto.com/ivannna;
page 18, ©Nature Picture Library/Alamy; pages 20 and 22, ©Karin Duthie/Alamy

Map by XNR Productions Inc.
Please note: Our map is as up-to-date as possible at the time of publication.

Library of Congress Cataloging-in-Publication Data
Somervill, Barbara A.
  Small indian mongoose / by Barbara A. Somervill.
      p. cm.—(Animal invaders)
  Includes bibliographical references and index.
  ISBN-13: 978-1-60279-630-0
  ISBN-10: 1-60279-630-0
  1. Small Asian mongoose—Juvenile literature. 2. Introduced
mammals—Juvenile literature. I. Title. II. Series.
  QL737.C235S66 2010
  599.74'2—dc22   2009028179

Cherry Lake Publishing would like to acknowledge
the work of The Partnership for 21st Century Skills.
Please visit *www.21stcenturyskills.org* for more information.

Printed in the United States of America
Corporate Graphics Inc.
January 2010
CLSP06

TABLE OF CONTENTS

CHAPTER ONE
WHAT IS THAT CRITTER?

A family hikes in El Yunque National Forest in Puerto Rico. They see an animal dart across the path with a small bird in its mouth. The animal is so quick that it looks

Invasive mongooses are a serious threat to native birds.

like a brown blur. It could be a rat or a cat, but it is not. It is a small Indian mongoose. This animal invader is living half a world away from its native **habitat**.

Birdwatchers travel to Hawaii to see albatrosses, petrels, and frigate birds. They go to the islands of Hawaii, Maui, and Molokai and see nothing. "Go to Lanai if you want to see native seabirds," says a park ranger. "There are no mongooses on Lanai." The birdwatchers cannot imagine what mongooses have to do with seabirds. The ranger frowns as he explains, "The mongooses raid bird nests and eat eggs. They also eat young birds and mothers sitting on the nests. Mongooses are destroying the native animal populations of the Hawaiian Islands."

For a long time, Lanai and Kauai were the only Hawaiian Islands that were not overrun by small Indian mongooses. A mongoose was recently spotted on Kauai, though. That sighting could spell doom for many animal species there.

On the island of Jamaica, a cat delivers a litter of kittens at the edge of a tropical forest. Unfortunately, a family of small Indian mongooses lives in a burrow nearby. The mother mongoose is hungry. She needs to eat regularly to produce enough milk for her three pups. She finds the kittens and eats two of them. This seems horrible, but it is a way of life for **predators**. Predators hunt for their food. And for mongooses, any food will do.

LEARNING & INNOVATION SKILLS

During the 19th century, British settlers introduced rabbits and foxes to Australia. The rabbit and fox populations grew out of control. These two species spread diseases. They caused millions of dollars in damage. People did not learn from these mistakes. During the 19th and 20th centuries, humans continued to purposely introduce species into new homes. This includes the small Indian mongoose. What do you think about intentionally introducing invasive species where you live? What problems might that cause?

The small Indian mongoose is an **invasive species**. Many invasive species arrive in their new homes by chance. This was not the case with small Indian mongooses. Sugarcane **plantation** owners had serious problems with rats. They wanted a **biological control** to get rid of them. Small Indian mongooses seemed like the solution to their problem. Unfortunately, the plantation owners forgot something important. Rats are active at night. Small Indian mongooses hunt during the day. A daylight predator will not hunt animals that roam at night.

The small Indian Mongoose has become a problem everywhere it has been introduced.

Plantation owners were not trying to create an **environmental** disaster, but they did. The International Union for Conservation of Nature (IUCN) studies these issues. It lists the small Indian mongoose as one of the 100 worst invasive species in the world. Some of these species invaded by accident. But many are the result of human mistakes.

CHAPTER TWO
ALL ABOUT SMALL INDIAN MONGOOSES

Two mongooses slip out of a hollow log. They jump and dance around. They chase each other and play like good friends. By nature, small Indian mongooses are fun loving. After they

Mongoose mothers use their tongues to clean their young.

are done playing, the mongooses lie in the sun to rest. One stretches and begins to scratch at the other's fur. It gets rid of insects hiding in the fur. Like monkeys and chimpanzees, mongooses show friendship through play and grooming.

A 1-year-old female mongoose mates with a male. She becomes pregnant and delivers a litter of pups about 6 weeks later. Although she is very young, she has already produced 2 other litters. There are 1 to 3 pups in the average mongoose litter. They drink their mother's milk for about 5 weeks. By the time the females are 10 months old, they can begin to have pups of their own.

One female can produce about 40 pups during her life-time. Of those pups, about 10 females live to become adults. Each of those 10 females produces 40 pups. That totals 400 mongooses. One hundred of those 400 go on to produce 40 pups each. That adds up to 4,000 pups. In less than 10 years, the original female could be the great grandmother of 4,000 mongoose pups.

Mongooses in the wild live about 4 years. On islands with plenty of food and no predators, they can live longer. The longer they live, the more babies they produce. It is no wonder that small Indian mongooses have become a huge problem.

A mongoose is about twice the size of a squirrel. The body of an average male mongoose, including the head, measures 13.2 inches (33.5 centimeters) long. The tail measures 9.5 inches (24.1 cm). The average female has a body that is

12 inches (30 cm) long and a 9.9 inch (22.3 cm) tail. Small Indian mongooses usually weigh between 14 and 23 ounces (400 and 650 grams). Most are small and thin. Females typically weigh less than males.

Mongoose fur ranges in color from pale grayish tan to darker shades of brown. The fur is lighter on the belly than on the back. The tail is so fluffy that it is nearly as wide as the body. A mongoose's teeth are sharp. So are the five curved

A mongoose's long, fluffy tail is one of its most recognizable traits.

claws on each foot. Their teeth and claws are important tools for hunting and eating.

LIFE & CAREER SKILLS

One way to learn more about animal behavior is to study a species in a zoo or animal preserve. Scientists who study animals are **zoologists**. They attend college and get advanced degrees. Zoologists who study small Indian mongooses work for colleges and universities, government agencies, or **conservation** groups. Some also work for zoos or museums. Zoologists work part of the time in laboratories and part of the time watching wildlife outside. Which parts of this job interest you the most?

Mongooses are **opportunistic** feeders. They eat just about anything. This makes it easy for them to adapt to new places. They feed on insects, spiders, and snails. They also eat slugs, frogs, and toads. They attack birds in nests on the ground and in trees. After killing and eating a mother bird, a mongoose eats the bird's eggs or babies.

Mongooses also hunt larger prey, such as rats, rabbits, and lizards. Quick and athletic, mongooses often attack **venomous** snakes such as cobras. A mongoose darts in and nips at a snake until it can bite down right behind the head. Mongooses do not limit themselves to wild prey. They have been known to eat chickens on poultry farms. They will also attack small pets in backyards.

Mongooses are known for their ability to attack fearsome snakes.

Small Indian mongooses are native to the Middle East and southern Asia. Their native range stretches from Iran east to southern China and south to Malaysia. Mongooses are found in tropical jungles, grasslands, wetlands, and dry forests. They are burrowing animals that prefer dry, warm homes.

Mongooses often dig their own burrows. They are also known to take over empty burrows when the original owners have left. Male mongooses live alone once they become adults. Females form a family unit with their pups. The fathers have little to do with the family after they have mated with the females. The mother is responsible for feeding and caring for the young.

At just over 1 month old, mongooses begin eating meat and learning to hunt. They have short childhoods. Mongooses become adults before they are 1 year old. Their entire lives are occupied with hunting, eating, and producing more mongooses.

CHAPTER THREE
A GREAT IDEA . . .
OR WAS IT?

When it comes to animal invasions, it is usually difficult to put the blame on a single person. That is not true for the small Indian mongoose invasion. The wrongdoer

Introducing the small Indian mongoose did not turn out to be as good an idea as people hoped.

in this case was W. B. Espeut. He was the owner of a Jamaican sugar plantation in the 1800s.

During the 1800s, sugar plantations sprang up around the Caribbean Sea. Slaves arrived on ships to work the plantations. Raw sugar was shipped to the United States and Great Britain to make rum. When ships pulled into ports, they brought rats. The rats left the ships to live and feed among the sugarcane plants. There was no way to control the thriving rat population. Millions of rats ate into sugar profits.

In 1872, Espeut had an idea. He knew that mongooses in India and Southeast Asia killed snakes and rats. Espeut decided to bring mongooses from India to Jamaica to control the rat population.

Espeut was very pleased with his plan. He published a paper claiming that the mongooses were a great success. Other sugar plantation owners on Caribbean islands and in Hawaii read Espeut's boasts. They believed his claims, even though the mongooses did not make much of an impact on the rat population.

Espeut began raising small Indian mongooses. Then he sold them to other plantation owners. In 1877, plantation owners in Antigua and Barbados bought groups of mongooses. In 1883, Espeut shipped mongooses to Hawaii, Maui, and Molokai in the Hawaiian Islands. By the 1890s, small Indian mongooses had also established populations on Hispaniola, St. Croix, St. Johns, St. Kitts, Puerto Rico, Cuba, and Trinidad. The Caribbean Islands were crawling with small Indian mongooses.

Perhaps if the mongooses had done a better job controlling the rats, their introduction might have made sense. Unfortunately, they were not as successful as Espeut had claimed. They killed some rats, but not nearly as many as sugar growers had hoped.

21ST CENTURY CONTENT

Every year, people make billions of dollars collecting animals and plants in one country and selling them in another. The Convention on International Trade in **Endangered** Species (CITES) works to control trade in endangered animals and plants. But what about animals and plants that are not endangered, such as mongooses, pythons, and boas? These species are bought and sold as pets and zoo animals. They, too, become animal invaders if released into the wild. Should the trade of these animals be stopped? How can governments prevent invasive species from entering their countries?

Different species of mongoose have fur in a variety of colors.

Rat populations increase quickly. A female may produce 4 to 6 litters a year. There are 6 to 12 babies in each litter. Even if many of the young do not survive, an active mother can produce 20 adult rats a year. During that year, her female young start producing babies by the time they are 3 months old.

It takes more than hungry mongooses to keep a population of rats under control.

And mongooses don't just hunt rats. The islands where they were introduced also had plenty of ground birds, frogs, snakes, toads, sea turtles, and lizards. Most native species on the islands could not protect themselves from mongooses. The mongooses ate nesting mother birds, their babies, and their eggs. They had no trouble climbing trees to catch prey. No species was safe from the clever mongooses.

CHAPTER FOUR
TOO MANY MONGOOSES

Animals have the same basic needs as humans. They need water, food, and shelter. Invasive species can easily adapt to new homes that have all of these things.

The small Indian mongooses' new island homes were ideal. The weather was mild. There were no predators to attack them. Food was everywhere. Well-fed mongooses grew

Without predators to keep the population under control, mongooses multiplied quickly.

rapidly. They produced many young. The mongoose population did not just grow—it exploded!

LIFE & CAREER SKILLS

For a long time, people did not notice the effects of pollution, over-hunting, habitat destruction, or invasive species. In the late 20th century, the environmental movement made people aware of these problems. New careers in environmental science, conservation, environmental law, and land management grew. People with jobs in these fields help us meet our need for a cleaner, safer environment. What careers in environmental safety interest you?

The mongoose population explosion affects island life in three major ways. First, the mongooses threaten the existence of native animals. Second, they are expensive pests. Finally, they spread deadly diseases.

The Hawaiian Islands have more endangered species per square mile than anywhere else in the world. The state bird, the *nene*, is just one of several dozen water and seabird species that are in danger of becoming extinct. Hungry mongooses have nearly destroyed the native populations of *nene*, albatrosses, and petrels in Hawaii. The mongooses have also affected sea turtle populations by eating eggs and hatchlings.

The small Indian mongoose has played a role in causing the extinction or endangered status of many native animals. This is true on every island where it is an animal invader. In Jamaica, mongooses have destroyed populations of Jamaican petrels and hawksbill sea turtles. Some birds are now critically endangered because of mongooses. These include Audubon shearwaters on the island of Mauritius and barred-wing rails on Fiji. Mongooses may be to blame for the extinction of a snake called the Hispaniola racer.

Mongooses will eat the eggs of turtles and other animals.

LEARNING & INNOVATION SKILLS

Plenty of cities have problems with rats, but they do not try to use mongooses to control them. The best way to control a rat population is to use a native biological control. Think of a city with a rat problem. What species already live in or near that city and prey on rats? Do you think those species would work as biological controls? Why or why not?

Mongooses also cause trouble for farmers. They slip past fences to prey on poultry. As mongoose populations grow, so do the losses. In 1994, mongooses cost the farmers of Japan's Amami-Ohshima island about $7,000. Three years later, the losses had risen to $110,000. And that is just one island.

Mongooses also carry diseases such as rabies and **leptospirosis**. Rabies is transferred by bites. Anyone bitten by a mongoose should be checked for rabies. The disease is life threatening. Victims need shots to prevent its effects.

Leptospirosis causes headaches, fever, muscle ache, and chills. It can even lead to brain, liver, or kidney failure. In Hawaii, people are warned not to swim in freshwater streams or pools. Many of these water sources are infected with leptospirosis from mongoose body waste.

CHAPTER FIVE

SOLVING THE MONGOOSE PROBLEM

The mongoose problem is serious. It is time to get it under control. This brings up many questions. How can the problem

No one has been able to stop the mongoose invader's population from growing.

be solved? How much will it cost? Where will the money come from? And, finally, will the solution work?

It should be easy. After all, the mongooses are on islands. That limits how far the mongooses can roam. Mongooses can be trapped. It is not as easy at it seems, though. In the 1990s, two towns on Amami-Ohshima island began trapping programs. Between 15 and 20 trappers were hired. Each had 10 to 30 mongoose traps. After 9 months, each trapper had captured more than 1,000 mongooses. This shows how huge the mongoose population had grown. The captured mongooses were only part of the total population. Scientists learned that the mongooses had expanded their range. To control the mongoose spread, a larger, more organized program was needed.

In 2000, Amami's Ministry of the Environment began an island-wide program. In the next 4 years, 9,960 mongooses were captured. During this time, trappers were paid a bounty for each mongoose they captured. The bounties cost the government a total of $268,000. The program reduced the mongoose population by 25%, but it was not enough to get the invaders under control.

While the trapping was underway, mongooses continued to have two or three litters of pups each year. They reproduced faster than the trappers could catch them. Amami-Ohshima is a small island with limited money to spend. Continuing the program was too expensive.

Other island nations have tried trapping and baiting to control mongooses. Trapping is only partly successful. It is a slow process. Mongooses reproduce too quickly for it to have much effect. Poisoned bait is not always successful, either. Using poison is tricky. There is no way to make sure the right animals are eating the bait. A poisoning program can end up killing endangered species and have little effect on mongooses.

The IUCN says that controlling small Indian mongoose invaders is a top priority. Efforts to reduce invasive mongoose

The small Indian mongoose will continue to cause problems until a way is found to remove it from the ecosystems it has invaded.

populations have failed. Control efforts, public health problems, and farm losses cost $50 million every year in Hawaii and Puerto Rico alone.

Damage to endangered species is an even greater problem. In Puerto Rico and the West Indies, the small Indian mongoose is linked to the extinction of seven species. Many other species on Caribbean and Pacific islands are now endangered or threatened because of small Indian mongooses. It is clear that introducing small Indian mongooses to control rats was a disaster. There are still plenty of rats. And there are far too many mongooses!

21ST CENTURY CONTENT

May 22 is the International Day for Biological Diversity (IDB). The day is dedicated to spreading knowledge and awareness of conservation issues throughout the world. In 2009, the IDB focused on invasive species. Invasive species are a concern for governments, businesses, and individuals. What could you do to help people understand more about invasive species?

NORTH AMERICA

GREAT BRITAIN

Korčula

UNITED STATES

Hawaii

area of inset

El Yunque Nat'l Forest

Hispaniola

CUBA

Puerto Rico

JAMAICA

St. John

Antigua

AFRICA

St. Croix

St. Kitts

BARBADOS

Caribbean Sea

Trinidad

PACIFIC OCEAN

ATLANTIC OCEAN

SOUTH AMERICA

FIJI ISLANDS

Kauai

Hawaii

Oahu

Niihau

Maui

Molokai

Kahoolawe

Hawaii

N
W   E
S

0   2000 mi
0   2000 km

This map shows where in the world small Indian mongooses live naturally and where they have invaded.

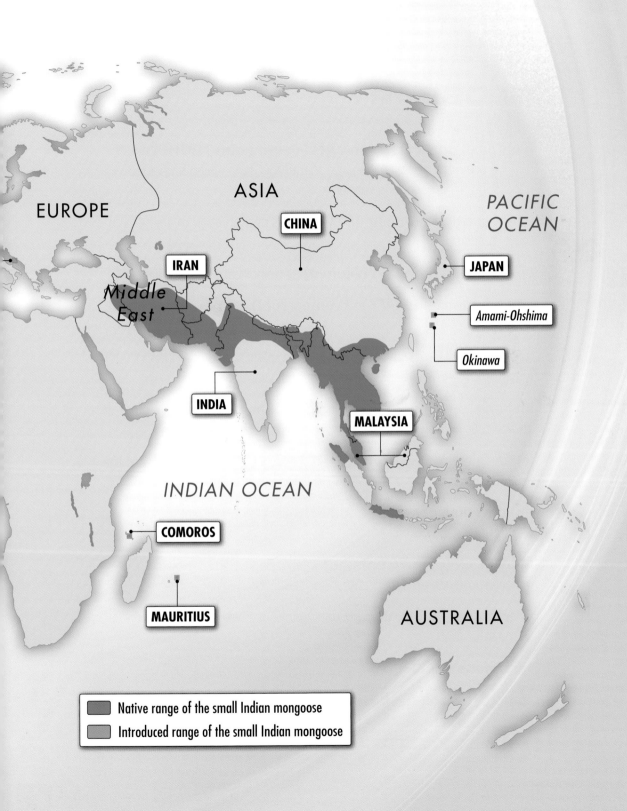

EUROPE

ASIA

PACIFIC OCEAN

CHINA

IRAN

Middle East

JAPAN

Amami-Ohshima

Okinawa

INDIA

MALAYSIA

INDIAN OCEAN

COMOROS

AUSTRALIA

MAURITIUS

■ Native range of the small Indian mongoose
■ Introduced range of the small Indian mongoose

GLOSSARY

biological control (by-oh-LAHJ-ih-kul kuhn-TROHL) a natural predator or other plant or animal that helps keep a species population from becoming too large

conservation (kon-sur-VAY-shuhn) preservation of animal and plant species

endangered (ehn-DAYN-juhrd) at risk of becoming extinct

environmental (en-VY-ruhn-men-tuhl) dealing with any aspect of nature

habitat (HAB-uh-tat) all the animals, plants, and conditions that make up the environment where an animal lives

invasive species (in-VAY-siv SPEE-sheez) a nonnative plant or animal that is likely to cause economic or environmental harm

leptospirosis (LEP-toh-spy-ROH-sis) a disease that affects the brain, liver, and kidneys

opportunistic (ahp-ur-too-NIHS-tik) taking advantage of a situation or condition

plantation (plan-TAY-shuhn) a farm dedicated to growing one major crop, such as sugar, cotton, or tobacco

predators (PRED-uh-turz) animals that hunt and kill other animals for food

venomous (VEN-uh-muhs) having or containing poison

zoologists (zoh-AH-luh-jihsts) people who study animals

FOR MORE INFORMATION

BOOKS

Collard, Sneed B., III. *Science Warriors: The Battle Against Invasive Species*. Boston: Houghton Mifflin Books for Children, 2008.

Halfmann, Janet. *Mongoose* (Nature's Predators). Detroit: KidHaven Press, 2005.

Pollock, Steve. *Ecology*. New York: DK Eyewitness Books, 2005.

WEB SITES

American Bird Conservancy: Mortality Threats to Birds
www.abcbirds.org/conservationissues/threats/invasives/ mongoose.html
Learn how the small Indian mongoose threatens the existence of birds in their native habitats.

Honolulu Zoo: Mongoose
www.honoluluzoo.org/mongoose.htm
Find out more about the small Indian mongoose, including its habits and diet.

Protecting Hawaii from Invasive Species
www.invasivespeciesinfo.gov/docs/council/HISC%20 Presentation.pdf
Learn how the state of Hawaii handles its unwanted invaders.

INDEX

ABOUT THE AUTHOR

Barbara Somervill writes children's nonfiction books on a variety of topics. Because she lived in Australia, where animal invaders abound, she finds investigating these "imported accidents" fascinating. Barbara takes conservation issues seriously. She is an avid recycler and an active member of several conservation organizations.